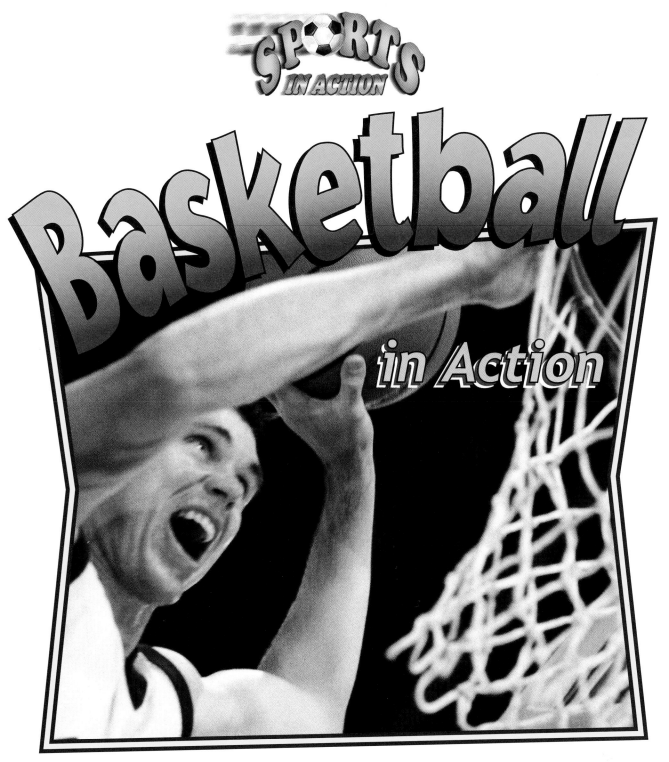

SPORTS IN ACTION

Basketball

in Action

John Crossingham & Sarah Dann

Crabtree Publishing Company

www.Crabtreebooks.com

Created by Bobbie Kalman

To Jarret Kramer and Erik Liddell—my teammates

Editor-in-Chief
Bobbie Kalman

Writing team
John Crossingham
Sarah Dann
Niki Walker

Managing editor
Lynda Hale

Editors
Kate Calder
Jane Lewis

Computer design
Lynda Hale
John Crossingham
Robert MacGregor (cover concept)

Consultant
Kim Mulkey-Robertson, Associate
Head Coach, Louisiana Tech
University Women's Basketball

Special thanks to
David T. Gagné; Andrew Corolis, Sandy Peters, Mary Bufalino, Amira Davies,
Ian Davies, Sarah Hopkins, Jimmy Kim, Andrew Ratkovsky, Anne Kubu,
Paul Lewis, and Ridley College; Independent Lake Camp; Blake Malcolm
Every reasonable effort has been made in obtaining authorization, where
necessary, to publish images of the athletes who appear in this book. The
publishers would be pleased to have any oversights or omissions brought
to their attention so that they may be corrected for subsequent printings.

Photographs and reproductions
Marc Crabtree: pages 8, 14, 15 (both), 18, 18-19, 25 (both), 27, 29 (bottom);
Bobbie Kalman: page 29 (top); Rod Scapillati/Ridley College Archives: pages
9, 28; Michael Zito/SportsChrome: page 10; other images by Digital Stock and
Eyewire, Inc.

Illustrations
Trevor Morgan: pages 7, 11
Bonna Rouse: pages 6, 12-13, 15, 17, 19, 21, 22, 23, 27

Production coordinator
Hannelore Sotzek

Digital prepress
Embassy Graphics

Crabtree Publishing Company

PMB 16A
350 Fifth Avenue
Suite 3308
New York
N.Y. 10118

612 Welland Avenue
St. Catharines
Ontario, Canada
L2M 5V6

73 Lime Walk
Headington
Oxford OX3 7AD
United Kingdom

Cataloging in Publication Data
Crossingham, John
  Basketball in action

(Sports in action)
Includes index.

ISBN 0-7787-0162-X (library bound) ISBN 0-7787-0174-3 (pbk.)
This book introduces the techniques, equipment, rules, and safety
requirements of basketball.

1. Basketball—Juvenile literature. 2. Basketball—Training—Juvenile
literature. [1. Basketball.] I. Dann, Sarah, 1970- . II. Title. III. Series:
Kalman, Bobbie. Sports in action.

GV885.1.C76 2000   j796.323 21   LC 99-38042
                                                                              CIP

Contents

Wh t is Basketb ll?

Basketball is a fast-paced game that is exciting to play and watch. Players on two teams move the ball by **passing**, or throwing, it to one another or by **dribbling**, or bouncing, the ball as they move down the court. The object of the game is to score points by throwing the ball through the opponents' basket. The team that scores the most points wins the game.

Most basketball games are divided into four sections called **quarters** that are eight to twelve minutes in length. Some have only two 20-minute sections called **halves**. If the score is tied at the end of the game, teams play a five-minute period called **overtime**.

The history of the game

Basketball was invented during the winter of 1891 in Springfield, Massachusetts. James Naismith, an instructor at the YMCA training school, made up an indoor game to challenge his students because it was too cold to play outdoor sports. He hung a peach basket at either end of the gymnasium, and two teams of students tried to throw a soccer ball into the baskets. By the 1920s, a set of rules was written, which is similar to the one used today.

*When a player gets the ball through the hoop, it is called a **basket**. Most baskets are worth two points. A basket sunk from behind the **three-point arc** earns three points (see page 7). A successful **free throw** earns one point (see page 29).*

Order of the Court

Basketball is played on a rectangular playing surface called a court. The court boundaries are marked by lines and circles. Indoor courts have a smooth, hardwood floor. Outdoor courts are located on an area of pavement. Two baskets hang ten feet (3 m) off the ground, one at either end of the court. Each player on a basketball team plays a **position**, which means he or she has a specific job to do on a certain area of the court. Players work together to help their team win.

Offense or defense?

The team that has the ball and is trying to score is playing **offense**. The other team is playing **defense**. While on defense, players try to take possession of the ball. If they succeed, they begin to play offense. Teams switch between playing offense and defense many times during a game.

*Every basketball game starts with a **tip-off**, or a **jump ball** in the center circle. A player from each team stands on either side of the center line. The **referee**, or official, tosses the ball into the air, and the players jump up and try to tap it to a teammate. All other players must stay outside the center circle until the ball is touched.*

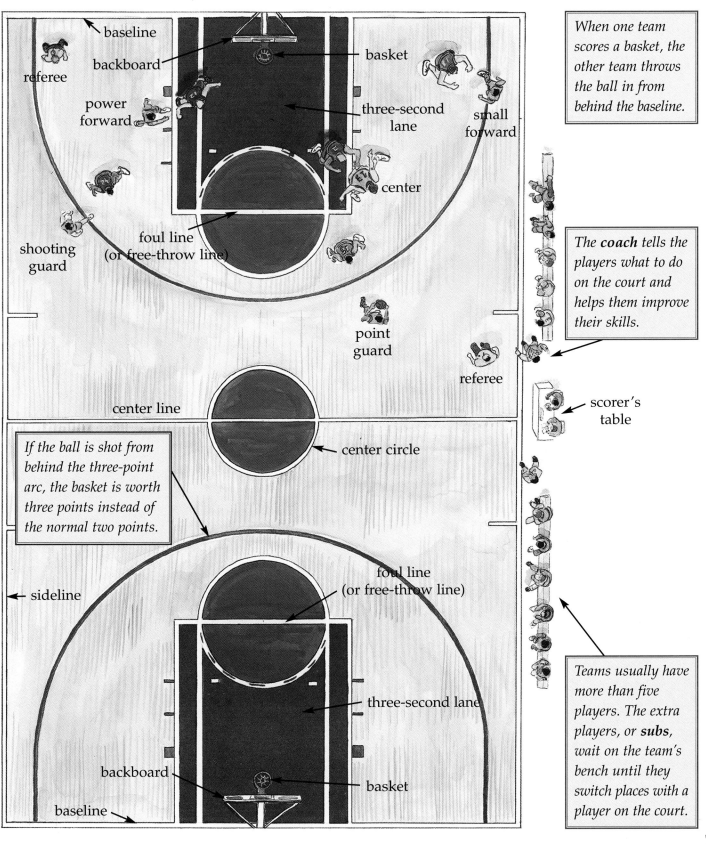

baseline

backboard

basket

referee

power forward

three-second lane

small forward

center

shooting guard

foul line (or free-throw line)

point guard

referee

center line

scorer's table

center circle

If the ball is shot from behind the three-point arc, the basket is worth three points instead of the normal two points.

foul line (or free-throw line)

sideline

three-second lane

backboard

basket

baseline

When one team scores a basket, the other team throws the ball in from behind the baseline.

*The **coach** tells the players what to do on the court and helps them improve their skills.*

*Teams usually have more than five players. The extra players, or **subs**, wait on the team's bench until they switch places with a player on the court.*

7

Take Your Position

There are five positions on a basketball team. There is a **point guard**, **shooting guard**, **small forward**, **power forward**, and **center**. Each position has different jobs to perform on the court. When the players work together, they can pass the ball, make shots, and prevent opponents from getting the ball.

Guards

The two guards are a team's best ball handlers. The point guard leads the team on the floor. He or she dribbles the ball up the court and passes it to teammates so they can take good shots. The shooting guard is skilled at making shots from all over the court.

*This point guard has the ball and is looking for an **open** teammate to whom he can pass it. A player is open if there are no opponents around him or her. A pass that enables a teammate to score a basket is called an **assist**.*

Forwards

Of the two forwards on the team, the small forward is the player that makes most of the shots at the basket. Like the shooting guard, he or she must be good at shooting from any place on the court. The power forward is the taller, stronger forward. During play, a power forward usually stays closer to the basket than the small forward. Power forwards help the center control the basket.

Center

The center is the tallest player on the team. Being tall helps the center win jump balls and make baskets. Centers get most of the **rebounds**, or missed shots, because they can reach up and grab the ball easily. The center shown in the picture is getting as close to the basket as possible to make a shot.

The officials

Referees make sure the players follow the rules. Many games have two referees. One watches the action near the basket while the other keeps an eye on the other players. A referee stops play by blowing a whistle. He or she makes many **calls**, or decisions, during the game. Players cannot argue with a referee's calls.

The Essentials

One of the best things about basketball is that you need only a few pieces of equipment in order to play the game—a basket, ball, and pair of basketball shoes. With these things, you can practice all of your basketball skills.

Basketball uniforms are made for motion! The **jerseys**, or shirts, are usually sleeveless so that the players' arms are free to pass and shoot the ball. Sleeveless jerseys also help players stay cool.

Players wear long, loose shorts. Loose shorts are comfortable and do not get in the way of movement.

Shoes are lightweight and have rubber soles for gripping the floor. Basketball shoes cover and support the ankle to help prevent injuries.

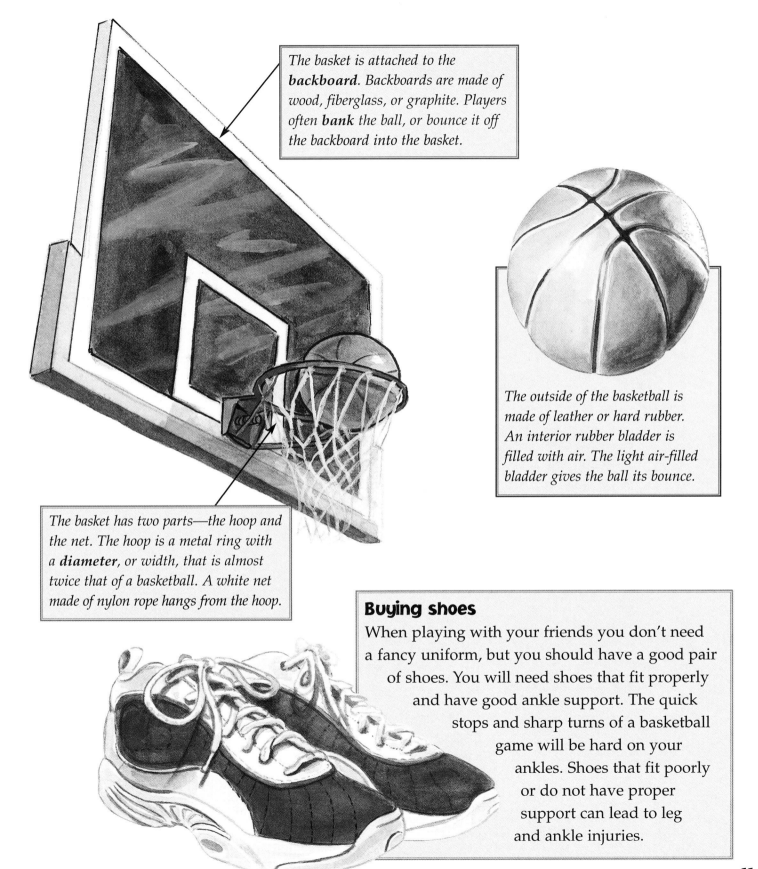

The basket is attached to the **backboard**. Backboards are made of wood, fiberglass, or graphite. Players often **bank** the ball, or bounce it off the backboard into the basket.

The outside of the basketball is made of leather or hard rubber. An interior rubber bladder is filled with air. The light air-filled bladder gives the ball its bounce.

The basket has two parts—the hoop and the net. The hoop is a metal ring with a **diameter**, or width, that is almost twice that of a basketball. A white net made of nylon rope hangs from the hoop.

Buying shoes

When playing with your friends you don't need a fancy uniform, but you should have a good pair of shoes. You will need shoes that fit properly and have good ankle support. The quick stops and sharp turns of a basketball game will be hard on your ankles. Shoes that fit poorly or do not have proper support can lead to leg and ankle injuries.

Warming Up

Basketball players can easily injure their feet, ankles, and legs. It is important to do a full body warm-up before you play basketball games or practice skills. Warming up helps your body get ready for running, jumping, and throwing and it also prevents injuries. Stretches should also be repeated after playing to keep your muscles from getting stiff. When you stretch, move slowly and do not bounce or stretch more than feels comfortable.

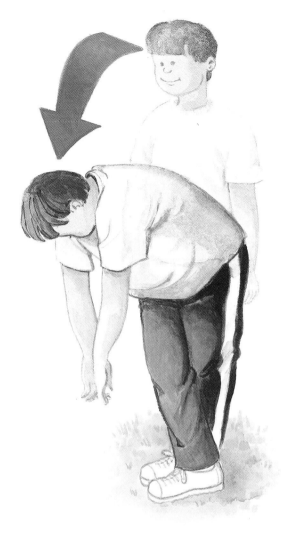

Leg crossovers
Stand with your legs crossed at the ankles. With your knees slightly bent, slowly bend forward and reach for your toes. Reach as far as you can and hold for five seconds. Re-cross your legs so that the one in back is now in front. Do five stretches on each leg.

Ankle stretch
Sit on the ground and bend one leg so that you can grab your foot. Gently move your foot in a circular motion, first in one direction and then in the other. Do ten circles each way, then switch legs.

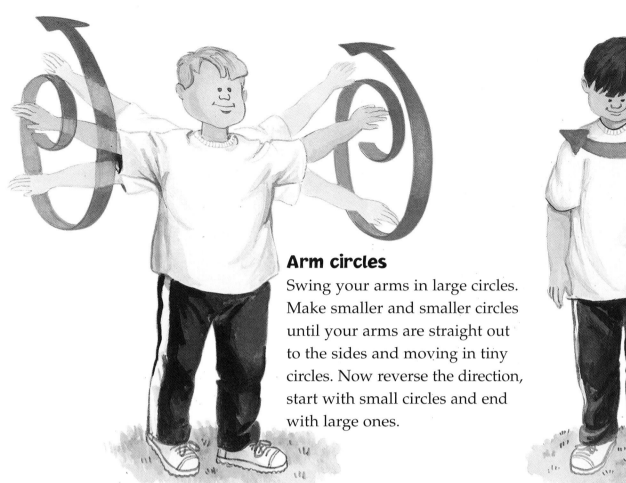

Arm circles

Swing your arms in large circles. Make smaller and smaller circles until your arms are straight out to the sides and moving in tiny circles. Now reverse the direction, start with small circles and end with large ones.

Neck stretch

It is easy to hurt your neck, so do this stretch carefully. Stand with your feet slightly apart, and tilt your head forward so that your chin points at your chest. Slowly move your head toward one shoulder and then the other. Do not roll your head backward. Do five stretches toward each shoulder.

Leg lunges

Stand with your feet far apart. Bend one knee and lunge to the side to stretch the inside of your straight leg. Hold the stretch for five seconds. Do five lunges on each side.

Dribbling 🏀

Imagine that you are on the court and have the ball. You are too far from the basket to make a shot. You look around but none of your teammates are open for a pass. What do you do? Dribble! Players dribble to keep control of the ball while they look for an opportunity to pass the ball to a teammate or make a shot on the basket. Keep your head up while dribbling so you can watch the other players on the court.

Dribbling don'ts

Be careful when you are moving with the ball. If you walk or run without dribbling, you are **traveling**. The referee will stop play and give your opponents the ball. When you stop dribbling, you have **killed your dribble**—you must now pass or shoot the ball. If you stop dribbling and then start again, the referee calls a **double dribble**, and gives the other team the ball.

Learning to dribble

Get to know how the ball moves when you dribble. Try dribbling the ball straight up and down and from side to side. Learn how hard you need to bounce the ball to keep your dribble controlled. When you feel comfortable dribbling on the spot, try dribbling while you walk or run. Can you dribble without looking at the ball?

(left) Straighten your arm and fingers as you push the ball downward.

(right) Raise your arm with the ball as it bounces up.

Pivot stepping

If you've killed your dribble, you can **pivot** to move away from an opponent and look for an open teammate. Plant one foot on the ground and keep it there—this is your **pivot foot**. Take a step with your other foot to rotate your body. Now you are ready to pass the ball! Make sure your pivot foot does not leave the floor or you will be called for traveling.

Passing

Players with good passing skills help their team gain more opportunities to shoot the ball at the basket. They must pass quickly and accurately to keep their opponents from stealing the ball. Remember that basketball is a team sport. If you can't move toward the basket or a teammate has a better chance to shoot than you do, pass the ball!

Try to pass the ball to your teammate at chest level. Chest passes are the easiest to catch.

Chest pass

The chest pass is a fast pass that works best when there is no one between the passer and receiver. To throw a chest pass, grasp the ball with both hands and pull it to your chest. Step forward and push the ball straight out toward your target. Your fingers should flick outward as the ball leaves your hands.

Bounce pass

The bounce pass is useful when there is an opponent between the passer and receiver. The ball falls beneath the opponent's hands and bounces to the receiver. Grasp the ball with both hands in front of your chest. While taking a step forward, throw the ball hard at the floor so that it bounces up into your teammate's hands.

Passing Drills

When you pass, you have to get the ball to your teammates while keeping it away from your opponents. Use these simple drills to help you learn how to control your passes and move the ball quickly to the player you choose.

Fast passes

Practice your passing skills with a friend. Stand four giant steps away from your partner. Pass the ball back and forth as quickly as you can without letting the ball bounce. Aim carefully so your partner will not have to move to receive your pass.

Step toward your target whenever you pass. Your passes will be more accurate.

Monkey-in-the-Middle

The best passes are the ones your opponents cannot touch! Play a game of monkey-in-the-middle with a group of four or more friends. Form a circle around one player, or the "monkey." The players in the circle have to pass the ball to each other without letting the monkey touch it. Use only chest and bounce passes. If the monkey touches the ball, he or she switches spots with the passer.

Switch it up

Stand three giant steps from your partner. To start, throw a chest pass to your partner and then have your partner throw a bounce pass to you. Repeat the throws, but this time you throw a bounce pass and your partner throws a chest pass. Continue until you each throw five passes in a row without missing or dropping the ball.

To make this drill more difficult, use two balls. Have one player throw a chest pass at the same time as the other player throws a bounce pass.

Shooting Gallery

When you are able to dribble and pass, you can learn the most exciting skill of all— shooting! Even though the hoop you are aiming for is almost twice as big as the ball, shooting is much harder than it looks. You must have excellent aim and know exactly how hard to throw the ball if you want to sink a basket. The key to shooting well is learning the right motion and then repeating it. Learn the shots on the following pages and soon you will be scoring points!

When shooting, put your shooting hand beneath the ball. Don't let the ball rest directly on your palm but hold it up with your fingers and thumb. Your other hand rests on the side of the ball to keep it balanced.

Jump shot

The **jump shot**, or **jumper,** is the most common and useful shot in basketball. You can shoot a jumper from almost anywhere on the court.

*A jump shot with a high **arc**, or curve, is difficult to block. The ball should move high into the air and then drop into the hoop.*

Allow the ball to roll off your fingertips to give it a backwards spin.

1. Bring the ball up in front of your forehead. Your shooting elbow points toward the basket. Your knees should be slightly bent with your shooting foot just ahead of your other foot. Your toes should face the basket.

2. Jump up, straighten your shooting arm, and release the ball toward the basket. Straighten the fingers and wrist of your shooting hand as you shoot. Be sure to **follow through**, or continue the shooting motion, after you release the ball.

The lay-up

A **lay-up** is the easiest shot to sink because you make it when you are close to the hoop. Players toss the ball against the backboard so that it banks into the basket.

1. Dribble the ball toward the basket until you are two big steps away. Take one large step with your right leg, and transfer the ball to your right hand. Keep your knees bent and your body low to the ground.

2. Step and spring off the floor with your left leg. Lift up your right knee and reach up with your right arm until it is straight while holding the ball in your palm.

3. Toss the ball up and toward the backboard so that it bounces off the backboard and into the basket. Bend your knees when you land.

These instructions are for a right-handed lay-up. To perform a left-handed lay-up, replace the above references with the opposite hand or foot.

22

Hook shot

The **hook shot** is a great way to shoot the ball over a tall defender who is between you and the basket. Hold out your left arm toward the defender to keep some distance between you. Hold the ball with your right hand and raise your arm in a sweeping motion over your head. Release the ball when your arm is straight above your head.

Slam dunk!

Everyone loves the excitement of a **slam dunk**! A player leaps up, slams the ball through the basket, and hangs from the hoop for a moment. Don't worry if you cannot reach the hoop to dunk. A dunk may be exciting, but it is also the least important shot in basketball. A good jump shooter can score more points than a great dunker!

Get the Boards

Did you miss your shot? Don't just stand there feeling disappointed—get the boards! Getting the boards is what coaches and players call **rebounding**, or grabbing the ball after a missed shot. Just like passing and dribbling, rebounding is important in helping your team keep control of the ball.

Follow the shot

Each time you make a jump shot, run toward the hoop and get ready to grab the rebound. Always be ready for a rebound because it may give you a second shot on the basket if you miss the first time. Watch how the ball bounces as it hits different parts of the basket and backboard. Knowing how the ball moves will help you be the first player to reach the ball.

Boxing out

In the pictures on this page, the player on the right is using an important skill called **boxing out**. As the shot went up, she moved in front of her opponent and faced the basket, as shown in the picture above. This move put her in position to grab the rebound, as shown right. The player behind her is boxed out because she cannot reach the ball over her opponent.

Defense!

The player in red is in a good defensive stance. He is standing with his legs apart and his arms stretched wide. In this position, he can make it difficult for his opponent to pass the ball or move past him.

Gaining control of the game when the other team has possession of the ball takes skill and hard work. When your opponents are trying to make baskets in your net, you have to focus on defense. Your team **guards**, or defends, the basket by keeping opponents from scoring and by getting possession of the ball.

Between the ball and the basket

To play defense, stay between your opponent and the basket. When guarding, keep your legs at least shoulder-width apart and slightly bent. Hold your arms up and out so that you are ready to block a pass or shot. Opponents will often move their head or the ball in one direction and then dribble in another. Keep your eyes on your opponent's midsection in order to follow his or her movements closely.

Stealing

When on defense, you can **intercept**, or grab, an opponent's pass. You can also try to take the ball while your opponent is dribbling. Be careful—you can't push or shove your opponent while trying to steal the ball.

As an opponent comes closer to the basket, this defender raises his arms to block her shot.

Steal Deal

This drill gives you and a friend the chance to dribble defensively and practice stealing. Mark a large square about two giant steps by two giant steps in size. Your partner dribbles the ball inside the square, and you try to steal it and take it outside the square. If you do, you get a point. When you have five points, switch places with your partner.

Fouls and Free Throws

Basketball is not a contact sport. Players are not allowed to push, hold, hit, or trip their opponents. The no-contact rule prevents players from unfairly interfering with a pass, shot, or dribble. Whenever contact between players is made, the referee quickly decides if is **illegal**, or not allowed. If it is illegal, the referee calls a **foul**.

Foul play

When one player fouls another player it is called a **personal foul**. Personal fouls are a common part of a game, and most happen by accident. Usually, they are committed by defense players who are trying to get the ball. Be careful—a player who receives five personal fouls during a game is **ejected**, or thrown out of the game.

An **intentional foul** is called when the referee feels that a player committed a personal foul on purpose. You can be ejected for committing a dangerous intentional foul. A **technical foul** is called when a player or coach behaves disrespectfully. Fighting or arguing with the referee or another player are all examples of disrespectful behavior.

Blocking or charging?

When a player with the ball knocks you over as he or she approaches the basket, who gets the foul? If you were standing still before the offensive player knocked you over, he or she would get a **charging** foul. If your feet were moving, however, you would be called for a **blocking** foul.

Take a shot

If you are fouled just as you shoot, you get two **free throws**, or shots at the basket. If you are fouled just as you score, you get a free throw plus the points from the basket. A successful free throw is worth one point. The player who was fouled shoots from behind the foul line. All other players stand outside the lane. They cannot move until the ball either hits or misses the basket.

During free throws, players from the team that committed the foul, shown here in blue shirts, stand closest to the basket.

The throw-in

A **throw-in** is used in three instances in basketball. When a team sends the ball out-of-bounds, the other team gets a throw-in from the spot where the ball went out. If you get fouled when you are not shooting, you are also awarded a throw-in. Finally, after a basket is scored, the other team gets a throw-in from the baseline. To perform a throw-in, hold the ball above your head and throw it to a teammate. Your feet are not allowed to go over the line as you throw.

Test Your Skills

You may not always have enough people to play a full game of basketball. Don't worry, you can still test your skills! If you have a ball, a basket, and a few friends there are many games you can play. Here are a few simple ones to try.

H-O-R-S-E

H-O-R-S-E is a shooting game that works best with four people.

1. Decide who will go first, second, third, and fourth.

2. The first player shoots the ball from any spot on the court. If he or she makes the basket, the rest of the players try to shoot the same shot from the same place. Each player who misses the basket gets a letter— "H" for is the first miss, "O" for the second, and so on.

3. If the first player misses the shot, the next player chooses a spot and tries to make a basket.

4. When a player misses five shots and gets all the letters in the word "H-O-R-S-E," he or she is out of the game. The winner is the last player remaining in the game.

Around the world

This game will help you work on taking shots all over the court.

1. Decide the shooting order of the players.
2. Beginning with the first player, each player takes a turn trying to shoot a basket from each of eight spots selected on a court.
3. If a player misses, he or she has two choices:
   a) stay at the spot and wait for his or her turn to shoot again.
   b) attempt a second shot. If the player misses the second shot, he or she must begin again at spot number 1!
4. Players continue shooting until someone can sink all eight shots in order.

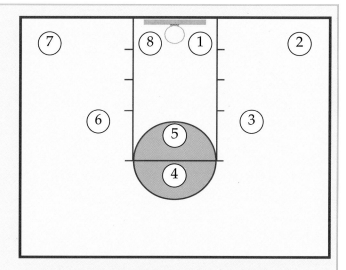

Here are some shot positions you could try for Around the World. If some of the shots are too hard or far away, try using five spots and move them closer to the basket.

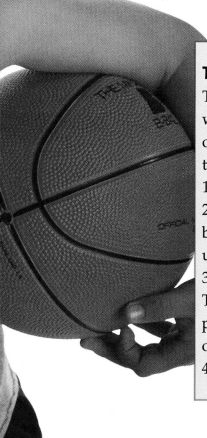

Twenty-one

This is one of the most popular warm-up games for basketball, and it will help you practice layups, jumpers, foul shots, and rebounding. You only need two or more players. In Twenty-one, free throws are worth two points. All other shots are worth one.

1. Decide the order in which players will shoot a basket.
2. Take turns shooting from the free throw line until someone makes a basket. The player who made the shot now gets to shoot free throws until he or she misses the basket.
3. Once the player misses, the other players take turns getting rebounds. Then they take the shot from the same spot where the ball is caught. Any player who makes his or her shot continues to shoot free throws until he or she misses.
4. Play continues until someone scores exactly 21 points.

Basketball Words

assist A pass to a teammate that leads to a basket

backboard The rectangular board to which the basket is attached

bounce pass A pass that bounces off the floor and up to the receiver

boxing out Blocking an opponent with your body to get a good rebounding position

chest pass A pass that is released from the hands at chest level

double dribble (1) The illegal act of dribbling, stopping, and then dribbling again; (2) The illegal act of using both hands to dribble the ball

dribble To bounce the ball off the floor

foul Illegal contact between players

free throw A one-point shot from the foul line that opponents are not allowed to block

hook shot A shot in which the player extends his or her arm overhead in a hooking motion

jump shot A shot in which the shooter leaps as he or she releases the ball; also called a jumper

lane Another term for the three-second lane

lay-up A shot taken next to the basket in which the backboard is used to bank the ball

overtime An extra time period of five minutes played if the score is tied at the end of the game

pivot To keep one foot planted on the floor and step around it with the other foot

rebound (n) A missed shot that bounces off the basket or backboard; (v) To go to the net and gain control of the ball after a missed shot

slam dunk A shot in which a player pushes the ball down through the basket

sub An extra player who waits on the bench to play; a shortform for the word substitute

three-point arc A semi-circular line that is usually nineteen feet and nine inches (6 m) from the basket

throw-in A pass from outside the boundary lines used to restart play

traveling Moving with the ball two steps or more without dribbling

Index

5 6 7 8 9 0   Printed in the U.S.A.   8 7 6 5 4